Drinking with O'Hara

BARRY SPACKS POETRY SERIES

Instead of Sadness by Catherine Abbey Hodges

Burning Down Disneyland by Kurt Olsson

Posthumous Noon by Aaron Baker

The Ghosts of Lost Animals by Michelle Bonczek Evory

Drinking with O'Hara by Glenn Freeman

Drinking with O'Hara

Poems

Glenn Freeman

Gunpowder Press • Santa Barbara
2020

© 2020 Glenn Freeman

Published by Gunpowder Press
David Starkey, Editor
PO Box 60035
Santa Barbara, CA 93160-0035

Author Photo: Sandra Louise Dyas

ISBN-13: 978-0-9986458-5-8

www.gunpowderpress.com

In memory of my mother, Lois Freeman

and

my first and best reader, Walter Butts

Acknowledgements

Many thanks to the following journals where some of these poems first appeared, some in very different forms:

Able Muse: "On Moving One More Time"
Connotation Press Online: "Love" and "On Learning Denis Johnson has Died"
The Cortland Review: "I'm Thinking"
Under a Warm Green Linden: "14 Notebook Fragments After My Mother Died"
Kestrel: "On How to Say It Best"
Main Street Rag: "Oh Yeah!" and "Paean"
The MacGuffin: "Untying the Knot"
Misfit: "Marwencol," and "Advice for a Graduating Student"
Nine Muses: "Ted Berrigan Steps into My Dream Again" and "Pawn Shop"
Prick of the Spindle: "Photo Album"
Rattle: "Hemidemisemiquaver"
The Road Not Taken: "Black Friday in the Pines"
The Same Press: "Ode to the Little Things"
Thrush: "O'Hara Late in the Day"
Unlost: "Artness," and "Syllabus for a Class on Modernism"
Verse-Virtual: "Mimus Polyglottos"

"The Past" and "Lightning Over the Interstate" were both included in *Traveling Light*, a limited edition from Wordtech Communications.

I am grateful for my family and friends who have supported, encouraged and inspired me. Special thanks to my colleagues and friends Rebecca Entel, Jen Rouse, and Shena McAuliffe. Thanks to my many amazing students who never fail to inspire me. And, as ever, my love and gratitude to MB.

Thanks also to support from the Iowa Arts Council, and to the Vermont Studio Center and the Tofte Lake Center for Interdisciplinary Arts where some of this material first took shape.

Contents

Fierce Love	10

*

Haiku for the Times	15
Artness	16
Syllabus for a Class on Modernism: An Erasure	17
On How to Say It Best	18
How My Students Convert Me	19
On the New Style	20

*

Invisible Cities: a Cento from Italo Calvino	22
Photo Album	23
Still Life with Vase of Flowers Cut from Our Garden	24
Lamentation & Charm	25
Prayer is a Mouth	26
Internet Word of the Day: Hemidemisemiquaver	28
Soup	29
Oh Yeah!	31
Iowa City; July Night	32

*

Paean	34
Dinner on the Patio, Solstice, Port Townsend	35
Ode to the Little Things	37
How the Painter Envisions Her Own Death	38
Fourteen Notebook Fragments after My Mother's Death	39
Alphabetical	41
The Book of Broken Things	43
Marwencol: An Erasure	44

*

Mimus Polyglottos	46
O'Hara Late in the Day	47
Sonnet Composed of First Lines of Ted Berrigan Sonnets	48
I'm Thinking	49
On the Wrack and Redemption of Olena Kalytiak Davis Using (in Generally Random Order) Some of Her Own Words	51
This Book of Ours: A Sonnet Composed of Last Lines from Marianne Boruch's *The Book of Hours*	52
Ted Berrigan Steps Into My Dream Once Again	53
Untying the Knot	54

*

The Simple Life	56
Daffodil	57
Late August Farmer's Market, Minneapolis	59
All Soul's Day	61
November Dawn	62
Black Friday in the Pines	63
Easter 2019	64

*

On Moving One More Time	68
The Past	69
Lightning over the Interstate	71
Advice for a Graduating College Student	73
On Hearing Denis Johnson Has Died	74
Negative Capability: Thoughts on Learning a Former Student Committed Suicide	76
Pawn Shop	79
Otters in the Pacific	80
Love	81

*

Fierce Love

for Vaughan

The bar's packed, but the woman
who's been crying for 15 minutes

while her husband yells at her
is upset she can't get a drink

fast enough when he's gone
to the bathroom and turns to me

for confirmation: *You can't get a drink
either?* but I'm in no rush and tell her so.

You're ok with this service? It's busy I tell her.
She asks if I'm from here, as if I'm an alien

she can't quite understand. I'm a writer,
I say, in town for a conference.

Ah, she says looking around,
so you're all used to settling for less.

Less of what? I ask, and though
she's clearly beyond her limit,

she's got it in her head we don't get published
where we want, don't get recognized,

don't make money. I ignore the irony
of her tears and simply say yes

we don't get what we want, but who
does? I say we work hard

to be the best writers we can, but
what life isn't worth the effort?

Settle for less? I tell her, yes, I want
more. I want a life where every taste,

every touch, stays alive and shimmers
on the page, where I can give attention

to the love and small acts of compassion
around me. I say yes,

I may never get there. I say yes,
I struggle to mean

the words I say, words like *tenderness*,
a word, like poetry, for which

the world, I fear,
has too little time, too little concern.

I nod to the bartender
to bring her another and put a ten

in the well as if to make some point
not worth making. When the husband returns

I can't hear them, but
her lips say she's afraid

she's offended me, and he,
clearly loud enough for me to hear,

says *who the fuck cares
about him?* Exactly, I think.

Once, I tried to watch
a youtube video of the Bataclan

massacre and found myself
embarrassed to realize

I was watching Samuel Jackson
on a Capitol One ad

before I could even see
the images no one should even want

to see. Outside it's Chicago.
Outside it's cold. Outside

three more were murdered today.
Who the fuck cares about him?

Exactly. And I thought
there is only one word

I can conjure
fierce enough to answer.

*

Haiku for the Times

Ask how we make art
in the face of times like these.
Ask how can we not.

Artness

an erasure of Dean Young's The Art of Recklessness

Let us suppose the impossible. Let us
forget ourselves. The nagging intention
always intends otherwise. Pay attention
and reconceive the fuel. We should fess up,
forgive ourselves, whisper the names of the dead
like clouds under waves. Desire always becomes
authority, music and incantation: *One
fish, two fish*: the words are ahead
of the self's multiplication, the life-
affirming perversity. We begin
to speak as verbs, a constant flickering.
Evolution doesn't solve problems; it finds,
fits, makes do. Toto pulls back the curtain:
It is impossible *not* to make something.

Syllabus for a Class on Modernism: An Erasure

When does the modern begin? The word
is always defined in relation, the same frame
but not without an audience. Tanks and planes
and poison gas: into the unfiltered,
the insurgent throb. Rites and myths come in-
to god: cinema, radio, new drugs;
Planck, Einstein, cityscape, polyglot:
influence is unknowable, golden,
and wholly other. Should art take its place?
The thing: a chiseled classicism?
The drama: a mental dreamscape? Expect him
to indicate the untranslatable:
no finish; dashes rather than prose.
Very well, the rapture selects her focus.

On How to Say It Best

a teaching philosophy erasure

My philosophy is in the vein.
It's true, every discipline must submit.
You know I lean on the same concrete.
Want wears me out. The bar in which I grade
takes into account the supple boundaries.
I cross my fingers in a kind of prayer.
It's like counting to zero. I'm able
to feel unfinished. You should know this.
No instrument will say what we are made
of. Excavation and re-creation.
I have ample classroom, but most of them
hide. I mentor the blossom; embrace the mode.
Make the concept my expectation.
The goal is to leave the classroom.

How My Students Convert Me

with thanks to Lily Hoang

One student tells me she cannot write
magic. One student on the last day
crying. One student walks us through doorways,
the geography of the zodiac, bright
stars knitting a story of dandelion
boys, a story of feathered snakes; one sketches
a tarot card; one speaks breathless
the first story he's made to call his own.
I learn of the travail of foxes, the elegiac
speech of pampered souls, blue margins, eternal
return, etc. One was verbal;
one refused communication; one made magic-
bearing fortune cookies. One softened
without admitting. One sewed money into coffins.

On the New Style

The new style will not be sentimental.
The new style will be written with no one there.
The irony will be written without scare
quotes or long digressions into the personal.
It is all true. It is all confession.
But no one knows anymore who is speaking
to whom. The new style is seeking
patterns in the fragments, some obsession
with pieces & parts & shattered questions.
You aren't taking me seriously
are you? The new style doesn't want to be taken seriously.
It's all just an unending series of questions & indiscretions:
the new style judges nothing, not even
whatever it is you want to believe in.

*

Invisible Cities

A cento from Italo Calvino

newly arrived and quite ignorant
of the languages, the connections between
one element and another could have various meanings.
a quiver filled with arrows could indicate
the void not filled with words:
you wander through thought, become lost,
enjoy the cool air. words replace first
exclamations, isolated nouns, dry verbs,
metaphors & tropes. the foreigner learned to speak
the emperor's language to be sure,
words more useful than objects and gesture,
mute commentary, palms out, straight or oblique:
as the vocabulary of things was renewed with new samples,
most of the time they sat silent

Photo Album

Here is the inhabited kingdom, the blind
metaphor, horse-drawn carriages in
the park, light on broken glass. A bitter wind
howls down avenues I've never seen.
Fond memories of moments that disappear
like light across a canvas, the memory
and the moment side by side. No one lives here
anymore; no design controls the scene.
Peeling paint. Dust in the corners. Owls roost
in the maple boughs; vines crawl up the white
walls in an Instagram haze: each produced
memory unfolds into fuzzy light.
There are always leaves on the ground; always
sunlight misted into haze, mirrors blurred into doorways.

Still Life with Vase of Flowers Cut from Our Garden

Flow
ers in
brown
bott
le in
sun
light in
morn
ing kitch
en glow
& coff
ee steam
and you
and i
awake
like pet
als turn
ing toward
the sun

Lamentation & Charm

A dance of cranes;
        a piteousness of doves;
eagles convocate,
        while cormorants gulp.
Birds in the indigo sky—
        cerulean
blue, the azure,
        the sapphire,
the turquoise & teal—
        where hawks boil
and finches charm.
        Tell me what you know
of the world,
        its words a kind of spell
larks exalt
        and magpies murder.
A bouquet,
        a bevy, a congress
and that setting sun,
        birds roosting. I do believe,
you've either seen it or not.
        Tangerine
& cantaloupe
        across the horizon—
you've either tasted
        this sky or not,
and all our birds winging home,
        or so I thought.

Prayer is a Mouth

with thanks to Robert Creeley

Eventually, as any theorist worth their weight
will tell you, all words break down, the poem
dissolves into sonic texture, pleasurable
but meaningless glitter
the way those galaxies reduced
to simple specks of twinkling light
above us have already died,
turned to some absence we won't see
for centuries. We know all this.
The question is how we keep moving,
keep talking and believing
in the words that we hear. You say sparrow,
I say finch. And we get by.
The word is like a dream where
you sit on a park bench tossing scraps
to the pigeons. The body
takes with it everything, its songs,
its dreams. A thin wafer,
a swig of wine: how can I pray
without believing the syllables? Today,
we've opened the windows for spring and my friend
whose mother is dying asked me
to pray for her. I wander the house enjoying
the breeze, a beer in one hand, book of poetry
in the other, reading Keats
to my cats. I want to say *hallowed*
but it sounds like *gallows*; I want
to say *inspiration* but it comes out

apparition. The syntax of empty moments.
The theorists all miss the point.
You say finch, I say sparrow.
Outside, I only hear singing.

Internet Word of the Day: Hemidemisemiquaver

Definition: A 64th Note

It's true I've always thought of Mary Poppins
with her supercalifragile thing
a bit absurd, a nonsense word to mean
nothing, nothing to say but the saying
itself a kind of music. But today I
learned this word with its specific meaning
that can only be said with a lilting
musical stride. Spell check won't recognize
it. Its own trotting gait is what it is.
Go ahead, say it without a little
lilt, a self-conscious kind of giggle
in your voice. When my wife is sad, she says
little ladle. For years, I couldn't put it
in a poem. Now it sounds just about right.

Soup

I called it *Our Lady
of Perpetual Wandering*.
Truth was, I'd followed
a recipe for a fall
soup called *Gypsy
Soup*—potatoes,
squash, chickpeas— in
a hippie restaurant
where we were free
to make decisions
like this on
our own, but when
I taped the label by
the tureen of hot soup
on the wood counter
where people made
salads, poured soups,
cut their own
desserts, everyone
asked what the soup
was, like, what's in it
and fumed when
I told them the name
says it all, I suppose
partially because
I was tired
of answering mundane
questions such as this
and wanted people
to look or smell

and decide without
my label. How else
can you eat without
expectation, the way
the world should come
to us, all of us.
Next time, I
will call it
soup. I will
pour you a bowl.
I will say
Here. Taste.

Oh Yeah!

for Mingus

If we could strip away the world's logic,
I'm sure we'd find a rhythm like this:
wave on top of wave, preposterous
and perfect, pounding on shore, a music

with its coast ever shifting, around, over, through—
prepositions without context, your voice
lost behind the din of its own chaos.
If we dig to where the rhythm runs true,

we would find your bass line, driving and driven,
swirling and syncopated, and you
buried in the mix, shouting and stuttering, a few
mumbles and groans. Your music will not forgive.

Relentless, it stops wordless in its tracks,
a pool of nouns longing for their syntax.

Iowa City; July Night

Would Kerouac listen to hip-hop now like he listened to jazz then? Summer's grape twilight silhouettes the buildings. On the street, flip flops and shiny spiked heels, the distant glow of cell phones and streetlights. Rumble of motorcycles and snippets of conversation—"So it was just a cry for help," "You know you have a map in your pocket"—blurred with the hum of a hundred cheap apartment air conditioners. And here the dark bar where Berryman long ago drank his way into the Dream Songs. The old Capitol and flag lit against the pale sky, singles chatting on phones, couples gesticulating, bare shoulders, shorts and skirts, and did I mention it's twilight and I'm falling in love with the city when this Cadillac pulls beside me blaring bass-shaking windows on the corner and I think of Kerouac, that moment on the bus asking the midwestern girl what she does on summer evenings and she says she sits on the porch eating popcorn and he'd have been glad as long as she did it with joy in her heart, and I wonder, Oh Iowa, do we hold this night with joy in our hearts, and if, were he here with us, would he listen with joy to the throbbing bass the way he jumped and strutted across the country to Dizzy and Monk—the sensual night unfolding like the road, like bugs in the headlights—would he know from bow down come rise up come dirty dishes and soapy water come fire and redemption come all the language I've forgotten forged in the heat of my long midwestern night: give me the real curve of flesh, the pulse and gristle of bass in a passing Cadillac, give me the inconsolable, the incomprehensible, the prehensile, give me that feeling I've gone looking for everywhere.

*

Paean

Praise the broken, the ruptured, the disconnected;
praise the grass overgrown, the dandelion
seeds drifting over every beautiful lawn.
Praise the sad, the worried, the infected
among us, the words we might use to heal,
the syntax of sorrow and grief inverted
into music. Praise the music. The departed
now wander through distant valleys we can't see
uttering words we may hear but can't recognize
as their voice. Praise all the deaf and blind
messages we receive, voices in the wind
carried toward us and away. Praise the cries
and moans, the dispossessed and damned,
all that reminds us how little we understand.

Dinner on the Patio, Solstice, Port Townsend

The waiter says
it takes a long time
to grow young
then opens the wine
and the three of us,
my wife and I
and the waiter,
breathe in the evening
air and glowing aroma
of rhododendron
hillsides, a breeze
rising up
from tidal flats
below. Epiphanies
have a way
of sounding
false, so I'll be
careful here, but
the purple hillside
and sky, the flickering
candle on the table,
the salt air
and spicy perfume
and this waiter who
now's become
our friend: I
cannot find a word
for the moment,
the wine
in our glasses

seems transcendent
trancelike
before the clatter
of dishes and cars
in the parking lot
remind us
that happiness
is fleeting, that
nothing endures
in the shape we found it.

Ode to the Little Things

for Curtis

A warm October afternoon on the phone
with my dying mother, a thousand miles away.
The autumn sun weakens. I pace the hallway
trying to comfort, while outside my friend
walks through my garden picking tomatoes
and basil. Pumpkins on porches, dust in the fields:
we see each other once a year, briefly
at best; lament the lack of time. Juncos
arrive the same day we see our last
hummingbird. Later, autumn mists
have settled on the vine, and on the deck's
railing, two cherry tomatoes sit cracked
and overripe, his reminder of what it means
to have ever tasted anything so sweet.

How the Painter Envisions Her Own Death

She sees a sailboat in the shadows
on the wall, its sails spread wide in both
directions. *You think I'm crazy*, she says,
but I don't. But then again I'm loth
to tell her I can't see it. She sees
a face, turned this way, then the other;
against the dark wall, there's flowers, a tree.
Write good poetry, she says, then my mother
mutters more I can't understand, sees more
I can't see. She sighs. *I guess it doesn't
really matter.* She nods. *There's a door.*
I begin to understand the design
of how we move on. Pain, it seems, is a kind
of solvent. *There's a door. It may be mine.*

Fourteen Notebook Fragments after My Mother's Death

1. Delayed flights. Missed connections. The Dr. has said we may not make it in time. Now the car my brother sent to pick us up has gone to Dulles instead of Reagan. My wife says relax. I say my mother is dying. I can't remember if I was good when her mother died. Death doesn't love democracy.
2. Hours by her bedside. Late at night, early morning, evening. We sit; we wait. In the afternoon, I drift to sleep on the couch. Somewhere in my dreams, I can hear nurses talking, the sterile beeps and blips of monitors in hallways, the fan's constant hum on my mother's flushed face. It seems as if there is no longer any there there. Everything is simply metaphor. For what, I know and do not know.
3. 6 AM. My mother wakes to a crystalline blue October sky. *My favorite time of day* she mutters. I realize I never knew that. *I don't want to see it again.*
4. She had said her goodbyes days before. She had left us. Her body, however, had other plans.
5. 3 AM one night, I leave to get some sleep. At the gate, a fox in the headlights. It stares me down then disappears. I know and do not know what to make of it.
6. Happy hour and my brother and I smuggle a few beers into the room. At the sound of tapping glasses, her brows raise. A slight smile.
7. In warm October light, I twirl a dried milkweed pod and watch the seeds lift into the blue. There is a pond. I know and do not know what to make of it.
8. I stare at shaded walls trying to see the images she sees, a painter watching the light in ways I couldn't comprehend. The irony, I thought, knowing that in my younger days it would have been me seeing things on the walls.
9. Afternoon sunshine beside the stream. Autumn leaves, cattails, and

squirrels. In a field of wildflowers gone to seed, I watch a fox hunt then disappear without a sound. I know and do not know what to make of this.

10. *Who is that?* she says with eyes suddenly wide. *Who's behind me?* She says with nothing but a wall behind her. I won't repeat myself.
11. One morning, I leave my father's apartment before daylight to be sure to be in my mom's room when the doctor makes his early morning rounds. I don't know what I wanted to know. Muffin and cup of coffee in hand, I walk out the door as my father's light comes on in his back room and I see him shuffling his slow shuffle, the befuddled sadness of now living alone even while she's alive. I should stop and talk with him, but I can't. God knows what I want to know.
12. I don't know how many times I can repeat myself.
13. The priest tells me my eulogy should be brief. It is, after all, about bringing people into the church, not about my mother. I want to say no. I want to tell him that he's not going to bring me into the church that way. But, then again, what should it matter to any of us.
14. My brother and I confirm the body. I wanted to say no. This was not her. The wrinkles and lines on her face that made her who she was all smoothed down to stone, the life ironed away. This was not her. But I knew they just wanted to confirm they weren't going to cremate someone else's mother. I know, I know. What should it matter to any of us.

Alphabetical

>   *for Sebastian Matthews*

I suppose because I share
some of my father's neuroses
for things in order—the man
whose version of playing
solitaire was to stack the deck
into suits from twos
to aces—I alphabetize
my books of poetry, sometimes
putting them in their place before
I've even broken a spine,
and so I find myself
in the company
of you & your father
together, side by side,
your *Miracle Day*
next to his *Time & Money*, and all
things jazz in between,
your *We
Generous* beside his
After All. I have a notepad
I borrowed from my father years ago,
From the Desk of... on which
I write random notes & scraps
to myself & find his name
on all the tidbits I find too late
to remember what I meant.
So odd, the formal feeling
of my Dad's insignia

and my nearly illegible
handwriting, the engineer
and the absent-minded poet.
There is no bookcase that holds us
both, no music playing
between us, and I wonder
what it must mean
for you to own
your father's name.

The Book of Broken Things

How we live
on the edge
of a shoe about
to drop. The lightbulb pops
into blackness; the gate's
hanging on one hinge.
The tire's flat, the mower
won't start, the penis
won't rise—we're talking
metaphor baby, allegory.
The bulldozer sits
motionless spewing smoke
in a pool of mud. In
his last years, Paul Klee's
body had almost frozen
in place, each movement
more painful than the last.
Yet still he kept painting
his angels, artistic
transformation itself
a symptom. Not sure
if it's the diagnosis
or a compensatory human
response. I'm no doctor.
But I do know
when things are broken.
We are beautiful; it's natural
to have our hearts
broken. We will be
forgiven our grandiose
beauty and all
we never quite complete.

Marwencol: An Erasure

On April 8, 2000, Mark Hogancamp was attacked by five men who beat him nearly to death. After nine days in a coma and forty days in the hospital, Mark was discharged with brain damage that left him little memory of his previous life. Unable to afford therapy, Mark creates his own by building "Marwencol," a 1/6-scale World War II-era Belgian town in his yard and populating it with dolls representing himself, his friends, and his attackers.

Inside my head there's a world
of tragedy and beauty. I try
to take something plastic
and make it as real
as what's in my head.
I feel safe in my town. I am
like the elephant in charge
of the peanuts. The hero
wears a slit chiffon dress.
There's danger out there;
people are real out there.
Where do I want this story
to go? The bad guy gets away
and it sucks. People
are real out there. Remember
to turn off the town. *I
love you.* That's how I say it.
Out loud so I can hear it.

*

Mimus Polyglottos

2 AM and there's a chorus outside your window:
day and night the mockingbirds sing,
gossip, and jabber without a song of their own.

From screech to warble to liquid tone,
the mockingbird's whistling
turns a single bird into a chorus on his own.

No doubt, he wants to make his presence known.
Conspicuous high on eaves or fence or line,
he imitates as if the song were a song of his own.

Through the night, his songs ring across town,
and day finds him just as loud, an aspiring
chorus of voices rising as if his own.

It's like this I think, the desire to clown
and fake our way into a song, to make something lasting
even without a song of our own.

Inside the mockingbird's song, an endless string
of borrowed voices, phrases and nouns
woven into a single voice, warbling all alone.
The mockingbird sings as if the song were his own.

O'Hara Late in the Day

I'm drinking with O'Hara in my office.
The fluorescent light is buzzing. The cold
twilight creeps steadily through the windows.
I'm reading O'Hara, ecstatic anguish,
cheeky nerve. So many syllables.
There are meetings I must attend, papers
that must be graded, students urged
toward greatness, but his haunting gaze
on the cover *dares me* to leave him behind.
The building empties and so does the bottle.
Alone. Just me and Frank. The only moral
is of silk cacophony and paper rhyme
rubbed against the heart. I am living
with O'Hara. *Go ahead*, he says, *say everything*.

Sonnet Composed of First Lines of Ted Berrigan Sonnets

stronger than alcohol, more great than song,
the bulbs burn phosphorescent, white.
go fly a kite he writes.
too many fucking mosquitoes under the blazing sun.
how strange to be gone in a minute:
the academy of the future is opening its doors.
the logic of grammar is not genuine   it shines forth
(clarity! clarity!) a semblance of motion, omniscience.
I am closing my window. tears silence the wind.
old prophets   help me to believe.
the withered leaves fly higher than dolls can see.
sleep half sleep half silence and with reasons
squawking a gala occasion, forgetting, and
how strange to be gone a minute! a man

I'm Thinking

~two versions of a sonnet in dialogue with Gerald Stern's "I Remember Galileo"

I.

I'm thinking about Gerald Stern's notion
that the mind is like a squirrel crossing
the highway, something about faith, about not stopping,
about fear grinding down our life. I'm in the garden
pulling the knots of long tangled roots
that have taken over the bed, and I'm thinking
the mind is like weeds, relentless. O, endless digging,
endless compost, endless substitutes
for what I'm trying to say. My student
says she thought that Stern had died. I'm thinking
the mind is like mycelium, dark tangled mass fruiting
after rain. The mind is not fluent
in its own language, its own capacity
to describe itself. Nothing happens organically.

II.

I'm thinking about Gerald Stern's notion that the mind is like
a squirrel weaving across the highway.
Galileo thought it like paper, say,
dancing in the wind, but Stern's turnpike
of the mind has a rodent caught crossing
beneath a semi, split seconds to survive,
breaking free into the open, to live
beyond such fear. But here I am thinking
about the mind as mycelium threading
its silent way below the surface,
clotting the soil with its possibilities, wordless,
fruiting after rain, the mushroom's persistent spreading.
Or I'm thinking maybe the mind is most like Gerald Stern.
One way or another, it will make itself heard.

On the Wrack and Redemption of Olena Kalytiak Davis Using (in Generally Random Order) Some of Her Own Words

rare reader, listen and be convinced: the soul
should not be multiplied needlessly
when I asked to be left alone, I didn't mean, like, now
your visions have always struck you as useless
do not confuse them by speaking
of the spite you do not want to risk
disappearing in the middle of a sentence
as if someone just handed me a bouquet made solely,
entirely of the absence of the word i have never told anybody: i
would have preferred to be misunderstood this life
this everything I long to write
and right my wrong to kiss you drunk
and kiss you stoned
i just wanted to say *meadow* once and really mean it

This Book of Ours: A Sonnet Composed of Last Lines from Marianne Boruch's *The Book of Hours*

Rubrics end best with a semi-colon;
little vast rooms of undoing.
I made everything; the hinge shuddering
up here. You didn't make me new to have reason.

What happens to a thought
come in quiet? I tried letting go
of the sentence midsentence. Sit still in a boat
and you swallow yourself whole. Once a tongue

and a mouth and anything you gave it.
The same dumb animal in her looking out
closed her eyes to that radiance again. The simplest zealot
practices doom, brilliant and meticulous at their poisons.

There'll be a cult, said god; earth will heave unreason
and I'll be some other thing.

Ted Berrigan Steps Into My Dream Once Again

Dawn and I am opening the doors. My small town is too loud.
The bolts have been greased.
The rain has frozen (the dawn diseased
with all its brown outlines gowned
in white, the trash cans & dreams
along the boulevard, coffee and bread,
and I was thinking instead
of how easy the promise seems
to be lost in the wind. All night
the academy of dreams opens its doors,
another drink with X or Y, more
conversation, but it seems our tears might
finally silence the wind. Everything eventually turns to stone.
Dawn and I am opening all the windows.

Untying the Knot

after Annie Dillard

The new season like a snakeskin lying
in a heap of leaves, like an exhibit
at a trial, circumstantial, whole but
tied into a knot with no beginning:
Here. Now. The seasons have no edges to grasp,
no beginning nor end, an ascending
spiral. Ice lingers far into the spring.
The snake has shed its skin on broken glass.
Migrating birds head south leaving fields
of insects and seeds, then reappear
in the snow. Killing frosts before the leaves
have turned: time is like a child's toy Slinky,
rolling along mountain ridges at random;
at any point, anything might happen.

*

The Simple Life

The Buddha says we find ourselves in the midst
of the ten thousand things. Chop wood, carry water, mow the lawn.
Lock the door before you leave. Don't forget.

The Buddha says it's simple. No left turns on red.
Check your mirrors before changing lanes;
things may be closer than they appear. Don't forget.

Check the map, the compass; recalibrate
every so often. Wake with the dawn,
lose yourself in the midst

of the mundane: turn on the coffee, feed the cat.
Sparks always rise. Like you, they're gone
before you know it. The Buddha says don't forget

to take out the garbage, turn off the lights.
Truth, the Buddha says, is like an owl soaring home at dawn,
a solitary figure disappearing in the mist:

the hour is getting late,
your bare feet cool on the dewy lawn.
You yourself will be mist.
The Buddha says it's simple. Don't forget.

Daffodil

The tender stalk,
green, leaning
toward the sun,
its tip, as if
swallowing
the sun it leans
toward, begins
to droop
under its own
weight like a
shepherd's hook,
bulging
brilliant yellow,
on the verge
of exploding
into its frilly cup,
all pollen and lace,
layered petals
opening,
and it gets hard
not to become
all Georgia O'Keefe
about it, to see
the flower becoming
the sensual body
opening
and longing, sunlight
shimmering
on the petals' canvas.
It's impossible

not to see
the furrowed world,
the plow and disc,
the burrowed life
now come to the light,
now standing
on hind legs as if
still spring-blind, sniffing
the air all coated
in pollen and sex
and golden light.
It's hard
not to make this
become and become
something more
than just
a day, to think
that life is nothing
but the urge
toward that solar
warmth, how
one day we
should be able
to get our own energy
straight
from the source
like plants, and
like them,
burst soon enough
into flower.

Late August Farmer's Market, Minneapolis

Peppers & pumpkins line the stalls,
habanero and hatch, beans and squash, buckets of bouquets, signs
above vendors' heads. Ecuadoran drums & flutes, light
slices through the crowd, brats on grills, wine
and beer, football on the radio, and I
wonder what language, what sustenance flowers

in the market, polenta on the grill, wheat flour
pizza. A chill brings out the first coats & shawls.
The percussive language of vendors I
can't translate in the rush of crowds, only signs
and strains of a beautiful music like wind
through chimes. The angled light

already announces the change, the burdens lighten
for just a moment, a new music flowering
in the improvisation of voices and vendors, wheels whining
from the bridge in harmony, hawkers singing in style.
An r&b band draws a crowd in one aisle, the beer in steins.
The mind is fleeting in what it clings to and I

wander through threads of sound and smell, the eye
landing on whatever feast it will, then moving with the light
across the stalls and parking lot and crowds, the early signs
of autumn and its changes, a new kind of flower
emerging like new words, new names, our voices stalled
as we try to capture the world's lush blossoming, rewind

the images, the memories, the single taste of wine
from some long-ago feast, every lush nuance entering the eye

like the world before words, at the center a still
and quiet music. How the mind transforms sounds to light,
the light to music, the aroma of the flower
into song. And this river of people, the luster & shine,

the melody and dance, no hard angle, no sine
function, no trigonometry, just the liquid movement, the wine
and music of celebration and harvest, the flower's
own reminder of its fleeting joy. Once I
wanted to be a painter, but the light
seemed to shift too fast, and the brush merely stalled

tracing the bounty's movement, in place of its signs a still
life when what's called for is the wine pouring, the light
flowering on crowds in motion, a rhythmic bond between the eye and the I.

All Soul's Day

Brittle leaves swirl and eddy around the house.
A feeble sun slips through the liminal sky. A train

rumbles in the distance, blasts its horn, then leaves on the breeze
tell of its passing. Church bells toll the hour.

There's whiskey in the glass, jazz on the radio, early twilight.
Brittle leaves skitter around the house.

We've masqueraded, confessed and atoned.
It's the time when the doors crack just a little more.

Outside, only the passing train and the shuddering leaves.
The clocks have turned back, blue twilight all day.

Apples and cinnamon, potatoes and kale. Outside
a few last leaves shiver in the breeze.

You can hear it long before you're aware, the low bass—
Chicago, Des Moines, Omaha—

coal and corn piled in cars, a passengerless train passing.
How long, I wonder, do we wait for a vision?

Our loved ones listing toward the sky in limbo.
The brittle leaves congregate, dance in sheltered spaces.

A horn blasts. Trees shudder. Only the breeze is left to tell of our passing.

November Dawn

The first dusting of snow and a wicked wind
whirls the last leaves skyward. Gray dawn
and the windchimes in a frenzy. Eggs on
the stove, coffee steaming, window blinds
shivering with the gusts. A young oak
pulls at its tether and I imagine
it years from now, leaning in its thick skin
to the south, gnarled and bent with wind and smoke
through the limbs. Starlings line up at feeders
despite our feeble attempts to scare them
away. It's mornings like this I wonder when
my life became what it is, its false starts, detours,
dead ends. Like plant cuttings on the sill, we grow
in jars of water, leaning toward the window.

Black Friday in the Pines

for Walter Butts

Somewhere mobs are shopping for deals on goods
that never last, crowds in their rituals
of consumption. Out here, oak leaves rattle
and shake in the drafts. An eagle scribes huge
spirals across a thin gray sky. Here in the pines,
heavy boughs shudder and whisper in the breeze;
cardinals, juncos, and chickadees
flit through leafless underbrush: such tiny,
delicate voices against the constant hum
of distant commerce. An early, wet snow
melts underfoot, but in the shadows
it resists: I think of your letters, typewritten
and filled with poems in your beautiful voice.
How stubbornly beautiful to see the world as verse.

Easter 2019

Swifts & swallows
      dart & dive
           through evening
    light.
Cardinals perch
      in the dense shrubbery.
           It's too early
    but still we wait
expectantly
      for the season's first
          fireflies
    to light
like apparitions
      under spruce
           or in the overgrown
      garden. Another month
at least, we'll hold our breath
      like our beer
          and wait, until
    one day,
one day.
      In Sri Lanka,
           over 200 dead,
    in Paris, Notre Dame
lies charred.
      So easy, this life
          in the garden.
      At least for us.
A few pale broccoli shoots
      stand against the wind,

                    sunflowers
               growing randomly
where birds have dropped
          their seeds. Louisiana
                    churches in charred
          ruins, a border militia
turning vigilante.
          Even the garden seems
                    too vulnerable
          a metaphor. Inside,
a bonsai tree stands
          pruned back
                    to only the essential,
          gnarled architecture
of trunk & limb, fierce
          & bare. I don't know
                    what grief
          does to us,
but there are days
          when the world seems possible
                    & impossible
          at the same time,
when we will go on,
          and we can't go on
                    at the same time.
          There are days I can only grieve,
and days when I can only love.
          Outside, the magnolia
                    begins its bounty
          of bloom. All of it,
all of this beauty
          reminds me

        it is only tenderness
    that will ever blossom
toward anything I'd love,
    like this world,
            to be part of.

*

On Moving One More Time

Late August begins to fall. Birch leaves swirl
in the neighbors' pool. Dried grass, flowers gone
to seed, sun angled lower on the lawn
each day. The scales begin to tip, the world
still weighted with summer's abundance, but
a stone more on the right and everything
shifts. I'd like to think I don't cling
to the past. I've cleaned the house and shut
it tight. Only two lawn chairs and a cooler
remain, some last seed scattered on the ground.
I'll drink a last beer, watch the birds and be
on my way. It's such an aimless future,
the way we're always leaving as if unbound
to this beautiful world, so weather-worn and shabby.

The Past

It's like the abandoned mansion
where I'd take her to prove myself
brave enough to be whatever
she wanted—the ancient building
standing in its own rubble with the black
air of rotten apples, wet dust
& bat shit, like moments
that never quite become what we think
but never quite disconnect.
One day, a careless cigarette
would burn that hulk of a building
into a pit of charred bricks some
future kid would stand on the edge of
trying to reconstruct the image
of a house he'd never seen, like nights
we'd climb the hill to Jacob's Auto
Salvage and sit in the back seat
of some accident's remains—smashed
windshields, matted wires—drinking
a six-pack & talking of everything except
what was on our mind, the full moon
of intimacy climbing like a headlight
the passengers may have seen
before spinning into the telephone pole,
the impotent warning of whatever
was about to hit. That summer,
after work at the country club, we'd meet
at the pool, climb the fence
and swim in the dark.
One night, sitting naked on the edge,

someone flicked on the pool lights
and the blue fluorescence wavering
underwater like the infinite, electric
possibilities I felt embraced by
now trapped us like deer
in the headlights. Sure, we escaped,
slipped beneath the gate
and ran laughing onto the perfect,
dewy grass of the 18th green.
That fall, we went on with our lives,
but the past stays with us like a kernel,
lodged inside the future
it nudges us toward, her hand
still pressed to my back.

Lightning over the Interstate

All day, Indiana
north to south, Gary
to Louisville, a highway
I hitched years
before, and now find myself
looking at every underpass
trying to see if I can spot
the one among the many
flat bridges that repeat
themselves, interchange
after interchange, where
I'd slept a fitful night
huddled between
beams, lightning
over the interstate.
But it would only be
conjecture, every memory
lodged too far back
in the many miles since,
the road surely reconstructed
since then anyway. Who knows
where I was. Tom Waits
sings about a grapefruit moon.
Corn fields dry
in a weak autumn sun,
landscape burnished
in harvest dust. Everything
looks the same, mile
after mile of flat land,
backroads rising just enough
to cross the interstate then back
into the flatness, buried

behind corn and soy. A column
of buzzards spirals
over the dried land, a swirling helix
black against a cirrus sky.
Pool halls, darts, a bucket
of Miller and this cowboy
had dropped me off
in the safest place
he could as the wind rose
across the plains and I
huddled, praying
to some god I've never prayed to
as the hail rained & pounded
pavement over my head.
Storms & dreams & a few
merciful moments of fitful sleep,
a warm beer in my backpack.
At dawn, the storm had cleared,
the highway glistening clean.
How I'd like
to clean my own slate
like that morning, like
an empty page
in the dawn, clear
it all away, back
to where the road
led somewhere fresh,
but there's always
some part of me
curled up
under every underpass
I pass under.

Advice for a Graduating College Student

I've taken him to the bar. On TVs around us:
the Cubs, Trump, Comey, Weather.
He's amazed to realize a Professor is someone
you can have a drink with. He's confused.
He's decided he wants to write.
He wants to wander a bit, and he thinks
I can help him find direction. But what
I really think he wants is someone
he can feel comfortable telling that
he's going to take acid at commencement.
He thinks it will clarify things. I say, no,
it will just make that cap & gown
seem all the more ridiculous. I say
the names of our sins will cling
to the stones we're tossing in the river.
What are things without their verbs?
I say nothing lasts, not even your confusion.
At the end of the bar, a man laughs.
I love your laugh, another man says, *It's
so* authentic! Innocence
is the willingness to let go
of your innocence. I say I've got advice
but it ain't what you think.
I say you want the real thing?
If you're going to catch fireflies,
don't forget to put holes in the lid.

On Hearing Denis Johnson Has Died

I'm fifteen and the beer cans and pop bottles
lining the stone wall have been shot, piles
of glass shards and shredded aluminum
now behind the wall. We'll set another round
and fire away, lacking all precision but making
up for it with volume, shoot long enough
and you'll hit your target. I don't know
why I'm thinking of this this morning
as your face streams down my facebook feed,
friends remembering when they first read
your poems. This is how news of loss
comes to us now. You asked once, why
bother writing something that I could say;
the page is for the unspeakable.
A gray drizzle and distant thunder.
Your dog-eared, water-stained books
line my shelves. With time, my friends
became good shots, but I never really
took to it. I was always clumsy and didn't
see the thrill my friends did. I chose to drink
instead. But it occurs to me that this morning's
memory isn't about shooting cans. No,
what actually came to mind was senior year,
my friend S and I in the watershed, drinking
and playing hooky as usual.
On the way down the mountain, his 1965
Mustang clipped a tree and tore off the right
fender, but we were so drunk
we barely registered the accident.
This was his love, a well-tended classic.

The car could still drive (good thing,
since we really couldn't) and we made it
to his house where in his distraught state
he grabbed his shotgun as if ready to use it
on himself. Drunk therapist I was,
I grabbed the gun, said, "You want to use it,
let's use it" not of course intending to,
just to shock him, but I hit the trigger
and no, I didn't shoot him, but I shot a hole
in his bedroom wall, shot flying into
his sister's closet and clothes. The gun was inches
from his face when it went off; only luck
kept him alive and my life barely changed.
Only luck. There, that's what it comes down to.
No one except for a handful of friends I don't even know
any more know this story. S cut a hole
around the shotgun hole in the drywall,
put a string around it and made
a big drywall necklace for me to wear
in my shame. He gave it to me at a party,
and I wore it for a minute, trying
to be the good guy, then wanted to scream,
*You were inches from dead fucker! Don't
turn me into the butt of your joke.* Shooting cans
seems easier. No one pours a good drink
anymore. The gun was inches from his face.
I tell no one, but now it's on the page.
It's a gray morning here, and I feel a bit
lost. I can almost see us turning into wind.

Negative Capability: Thoughts on Learning a Former Student Committed Suicide

I'd forgotten and I'm not sure what that says
about me. Or I can't really say I'd forgotten,

rather it wasn't in mind, for it turns out
I remember every detail of meeting with her

to discuss her manuscript, spring light
on the deck talking poetry & how to keep going,

always, as I said, to keep pushing into the unknown—
I remember knowing, like the pale gauzy clouds

over the skyline, that she was on the edge of something
and in my mind the edge was always good, all

to be desired, but we have to be careful I suppose:
for some the shore is better than the sea.

She took classes just for the love
of the word and the passion for writing, with which

she no doubt was overflowing, although I'm unsure
where the line between passion and obsession lies,

and, as her story proves, obsession's dangerous.
As Berryman said, you die not knowing. If you have to know,

don't write, though we all know what happened
to *him*. By the time we had a conference at my house,

sipping tea on the three-season porch, summer turning
to fall, she was fraying at the edges like a page

torn from a spiral notebook. She wasn't sure
how to handle the writing, everything it opened up,

but still I kept urging her on. Is it more important
to make the work, even as the life flames out

behind it? Once I would have thought so.
By the following spring, she was leaving messages,

condemning me to hell for what I'd done to her,
never saying it by name, but I knew

for pushing her to write poems. I was over my head.
I cut the connection and soon

I simply didn't hear from her. It's not
that I'd forgotten really, but finally got to not

thinking about it after months of haunting dreams
about what it means to help people write poems,

those bare, raw objects that turn into doors
into the unconscious, only returning to the memories

when I saw her name attached to a scholarship
in her memory. Forgetting and not

remembering seem like completely different acts,
the former more culpable when the memory should stay

alive in everything I do. I remember her in the café
one afternoon, fidgeting with a pencil and dog-eared

notebook trying to ask how to keep from losing herself
in the work, and I answered sincerely, yet in hindsight

perhaps a little cavalierly, that losing one's self is a good thing,
to be valued; it is impossible to overstate all that I didn't know.

Pawn Shop

When I looked at my guitar in the pawn shop—
its wood top nicked and worn—I dreamed of old
love letters in a drawer, faded pictures curled
in dust, a cemetery lined in moss.
Junkyard mountains of rusting cars, dogs
guarding the chain-link fence. I don't know
how much I got for the guitar, though
every day I strolled the aisles of goods
cast off, just to make sure it was still there.
What was any of it worth? The clocks
and watches, the sax and fiddle, boxes
of jewelry and stereos, racks of weather-
beaten clothes. In time, I bought it back.
In time, I learned what little I lack.

Otters in the Pacific

We're on the Olympic Peninsula, my wife and I, staring out at the gray Pacific. A gauzy sky spits rain. Otters in the surf, whales in the distance. A couple behind us are having a serious conversation, and though I'm trying not to listen, I can't *not* overhear one woman ask the other what she would do if she knew it were her last summer, and somehow I knew the question wasn't academic. I couldn't help ask myself the same question, and I thought *this* would be good. Perhaps I would come here. We're on the deck at the lodge, a happy hour beer, waiting for a table. The women are happy to learn we're watching otters with our binoculars. We offer them a look, but they refuse, seeming to take satisfaction in our delight watching them dip in and out of the waves, appearing and disappearing with joyful uncertainty.

Love

> *Love—what is it?*
> *Most natural pain killer there is.*
> *LOVE—*
> William Burroughs' final journal entry

It's not
that I'd call myself
an addict,
though not wanting
to name myself
as such
raises
as many questions
as it answers
addicted to what
I'd want to know
although
somewhere deep
in the reptile
brain I know
what it is
though I cannot
name it, not
the way
Burroughs
named his ultimate
addiction, lord
save me
from myself
you know I can't

keep the façade
I've worked so hard
to construct
the concrete and rebar
the gravel and glass
the pipes
and wires the whole
building in place
of the simple
foundation no
I am a caesura
in the shortened line
a breath
in the midst of
the ongoing world
the ten thousand
things said the
Buddha the water
the wood
the charred pit
where we gather
and toss our sins
like twigs
into the fire
that will not stop burning.

About the Poet

Glenn Freeman has published three books, *Fading Proofs* (2006), *Keeping the Tigers Behind Us* (2007), and *Traveling Light* (2011). His poems have been published in journals such as *Poetry*, *The Cimarron Review*, *Water-Stone Review*, *Able Muse*, and *Rattle*. He has degrees from Goddard College, Vermont College, and the University of Florida. He teaches writing and American literature and directs the low-residency MFA at Cornell College in Iowa.

Also from Gunpowder Press

The Tarnation of Faust: Poems by David Case

Mouth & Fruit: Poems by Chryss Yost

Shaping Water: Poems by Barry Spacks

Original Face: Poems by Jim Peterson

What Breathes Us: Santa Barbara Poets Laureate, 2005-2015
Edited by David Starkey

Unfinished City: Poems by Nan Cohen

Raft of Days: Poems by Catherine Abbey Hodges

and the Shoreline Voices Projects:

Buzz: Poets Respond to SWARM
Edited by Nancy Gifford and Chryss Yost

Rare Feathers: Poems on Birds & Art
Edited by Nancy Gifford, Chryss Yost, and George Yatchisin

To Give Life a Shape: Poems Inspired by the Santa Barbara Museum of Art
Edited by David Starkey and Chryss Yost

www.ingramcontent.com/pod-product-compliance
Lightning Source LLC
Chambersburg PA
CBHW020736020526
44118CB00033B/959